T0103931

Falling Higher

Reason to Believe

Andre J. Nel

iUniverse LLC
Bloomington

FALLING HIGHER
REASON TO BELIEVE

iUniverse books may be ordered through booksellers or by contacting:

iUniverse LLC
1663 Liberty Drive
Bloomington, IN 47403
www.iuniverse.com
1-800-Authors (1-800-288-4677)

ISBN: 978-1-4917-2704-1 (sc)
ISBN: 978-1-4917-2705-8 (e)

Printed in the United States of America.

iUniverse rev. date: 04/24/2014

*In the quest to find myself, the longing to know
my inner self, I encountered a lot of people and
a number of literature along the way.*

*I cannot adequately remember all of which authors and
literature I pinned down over the years to find the right
words as I was trying to describe what I felt in my soul.*

*I wish to express my sincere appreciation to any
such a number of people or literature.*

*To each and every-one contributing to this
quest, my undying love and gratitude.*

'I was lost and found, I had hit the ground
I was lost, but now I found
That I don't need no one, to survive
You've got to believe alone, you'll rise'

From the song 'Lost And Found' by Judas Priest ~
Tipton; Downing; Hill; Owens; Travis

---

*'If you discovered how one wheel in a clock turns, you
may speculate how the rest move, but you better leave
alone the question of who wound up the spring'
~ Ulrich J. Becker*

*'Believing that the first cell originated by chance
is like believing that a tornado, ripping through a
junkyard full of airplane parts, dismembered and
in disarray, could produce a Boeing 747'
~ Fred Hoyle*

*'You cannot solve a problem from the same
consciousness that created the problem'
~ Albert Einstein*

*'If there is any one secret of being successful, it lies in the
ability to get the other person's point of view and see things
from that person's angle as well as from your own'
~ Henry Ford*

*'Our thoughts are real forces of energy which create our reality.
By consciously choosing our thoughts we create our life!'
~ Hannes Dreyer*

*'Simplicity is the ultimate sophistication'
~ Leonardo Da Vinci*

*'There are no secrets, just unknown truths'
~ Ernest Holmes*

First of all, I would like to express a sincere welcome to each and every reader of this book.

But . . . Before we start I want to share a moment of your time.

I want you to take a quick peek at the *two squares inside the circles* on the back-cover of this book . . .

Well . . . What do you think?

Is one square lighter/darker than the other square?
Or,
Are both squares exactly the same color?

If you think that they are both exactly the same color, you will be absolutely correct, believe it or not.

Two *physically identical squares* are perceived as different subjective colors, because each has a different surrounding color.

To further illustrate how our minds perceived things, read the following sentences:

I cdnuolt blveiee taht I cluod aulaclty uesdnatnrd waht I was rdanieg.

The phaonmneal pweor of the hmuan mind, aoccdrnig to rscheearch at Cmabrigde Uinervtisy, it deosn't mttaer in waht oredr the ltteers in a wrod are, the olny iprmoatnt tihng is taht the frist and lsat ltteer be in the rghit pclae.

The rset can be a taotl mses and you can sitll raed it wouthit a porbelm.

Tihs is bucesae the hmaun mnid deos not raed ervey lteter by istlef, but the wrod as a wlohe.

Azamnig huh?

<u>WARNING:</u>

This book is probably not for you and you should pass on it . . .

. . . if you are not willing to be *OPEN-MINDED*

. . . if you do not be prepared to *EXAMINE, QUESTION or* at least *CHALLENGE some* of your *BELIEF SYSTEMS*

. . . if you expecting *INSTANT* results

. . . if you are one of those people who need to change your life *YESTERDAY*, but you do not want to put in the time and effort *TODAY*

. . . if you are satisfied with being in your *COMFORT ZONE*, like your current lifestyle and enjoy the way things are going for you right now

It has serious philosophical content and is not a replacement for any religion or religious practices.

This is not a magic wand.

Preface

Our lives are heavily influenced by the way we think and how our subconscious mind has been conditioned through life's experiences.

Every one of us can and should have the dynamic living that we deserve in all areas of our lives.

We do not need to understand the laws of physics to improve the powers infested in ourselves to develop and maintained a fulfilling life.

What does this mean?

It means that we can and do create our own reality.

This is more than just a mere way of positive thinking.

We have to feel and live it.

How can we do this?

It's a matter of choice.

So many of us all too often fall in with the crowd and instead of trusting our inner wisdom, our genius inside, we conform rather than question.

We can choose . . .

Rewarding relationships . . . fantastic health . . . financial riches . . . true purpose in life and a meaningful spiritual sense of connection with the Divine, GOD.

Is this possible?

Absolutely. Nobel Prize winning scientists like Einstein and Bohr proved that quantum physics teaches us . . .

- *We see what we expect to see*

- *We create what we expect to create in our life, positive or negative*

- *There is nothing Outside that is not created from with-In*

- *Certainty is determined by our IN-tention and not our AT-tention.*

My uncle Willie used to say . . .

'One can fool some of the people all the time, and one can fool all the people some of the time, but one can't fool all the people all the time'

. . . And, Then there are people that make things happen, the ones that watch things happened and those people who asked *'What happened?'*

You see, for me, I am of the opinion that;

- *It's not about being right or wrong*

- *It's not about blasphemy, ridicule and contempt, so let us put that aside here*

- *We ARE all part of the Divine. Most of us just don't really KNOW it*

- *It's about how much we are conditioned and how our minds interprets our beliefs that matters, not the objective reality of the situation*

- *This is how the spiritual dimension of religion, science and life comes alive every day*

- *It stops being a theory on a page or a sermon from a pulpit and becomes a living, breathing part of your being*

AND I believe this from the bottom of my Heart, Soul and *Mind*.

I personally developed a Power Formula specifically designed for a balanced, rewarding and meaningful life.

I call it . . .

The Falling Higher Formula ™

For me, this is the PROBLEM to the ANSWER.

And it is yours free, on the house, mahala, gratis and verniet.

All you have to do is to study it and apply its principles in your own life.

The Falling Higher Formula ™

$$\$ = M \left(\sqrt[4]{E^{tf} \, U^{pi}} \right) L$$

Sound difficult?

No Way! Once you know how, it is actually so simple that it is difficult.

In the next few chapters I will explain it all to you.

Index

To the Edge of the Universe

*'Most people live, whether physically, intellectually or
morally, in a very restricted circle of their potential being.
They make use of a very small portion of their possible
consciousness and of their soul's resources in general, much
like a man who out of his whole bodily organism should get
into a habit of using and moving only his little finger.'*

William James

THE MAJORITY OF PEOPLE do not consider our psyche as relevant
in recent modern society and in affect loses a very important
and vital source of guidance to the connection of the inner self.

Most of us just let life push us around.

Some will give up, some will push back, but most of us push back
against our job, our boss, the government or whatever cause or
excuse we will find in our lives, hoping for that big break that will
solve our problems.

For some people everyday life falls short of the ideal and instead
of questioning, life pushed us into submission, we conform to
society and assume that something is lacking.

When reality disappoints, we do not validate our expectations.

We rather re-double our efforts that promises to change our lives . . .

- . . . *working harder, getting a better/second job, spend more, work harder*

- . . . *wanting the easiest diet, pill, exercise routine, magic trick*

- . . . *searching for new meaning in religions, rituals, contents, books*

We need to get to know ourselves, find and reconnect with humanity again.

When we do, we will see, by dropping inflated and unrealistic expectations, we are able to achieve incredible things, using our God-given ingredients to set ourselves free in Mind, Body and Spirit.

Deep down in each and every one of us we are afraid of taking risks, but the fear of losing is greater than the excitement of winning.

Deep inside, we will know, we chose to play it safe.

I always wished to travel abroad and desired to do so for a long time but always said; *That's all very well, I will do it as soon as I can afford it but right now I must pay the bills.*

Real interesting discoveries of current brain research and human motivational studies has shown that for all practical purposes an imagined, visualized experience is almost the same as the real thing.

So . . .

I want you to take the opportunity right now and visualize yourself at this very moment in time, traveling through air at the *altitude of 10,000 meters and in access of 1,000 kilometers per hour* ground speed, both at the same time?

Does this sound far-fetched to you?

Not really. It actually is quite normal in this time and age we are living in, as thousands of people are doing it across the globe every second of the day.

Visualize yourself this very moment sitting in a modern day luxury airliner standing on the runway preparing for take-off, awaiting clearance from ground control.

Take a few seconds and make it real in your mind; make it detailed as if it is happening to you right now.

Enter the role and become it in your mind.

Looking out the window, the pressurized atmosphere inside the cabin is thick and tangible, quietly anticipating the moment before launch.

Somebody is talking softly, somebody dryly clearing his throat, the flight attendants adhere passively to the call in their seats, facing backwards, adding to the serenity of the moment.

You feel and hear the power and vibration of the jet engines coming alive, like an iron maiden shaking and willing her-self to launch into the unknown for the very first time.

I always, as only momentarily, experienced at the thrust of the airplane a sense of mixed emotions, ranging right through from awe to a little bit of sadness.

There is no turning back now, no stopping, no time to get off.

Silent contentment took over. This is out of your hands now. You are out of your league. You are in a different world.

Still looking out the window as the airplane accelerate down the runway, people seemed to fade.

As the plane lift off, only vehicles remained, silently crossing underneath on the interstate, sliding little cubicles to unknown destinies.

The higher you get the more the feeling that the aircraft is slowing down, as if all those power is not enough to get you up there.

Still reclining at an upward angle in your seat, the perspective you get in relation with speed verses distance might even seem that it is slipping slightly backwards.

Eventually settling in at 10,000 meters for the 18 hour flight from Houston, Texas to Dubai, time stood still.

Nothing seemed to move down there.

USA, Canada, Iceland, Britain, Norway, France, Germany, Russia, Israel.

Drinking in the bigger picture, you're trying to imagine if this is real or maybe just the vivid sensational effect of your second, double 'Jack Daniels' on the rocks.

18,000 kilometers—1,000 kilometers per hour—18 hours to go.

Let your mind start to wander . . .

The Pioneer 10 space craft launched into space by NASA in 1972 took 21 months to reached Jupiter a mere 1,000 million km from earth.

At estimated speeds of 20,000 km/h and more for a space craft, the Pioneer can reduce the 18 hours Dubai flight to less than an hour.

That will be pretty fast isn't it?

It can pretty much messed up quality 'Jack' time, though.

Imagine, if we can speed up this whole process to the speed of light?

Did you know that the speed of light is calculated at 300,000 kilometer per second?

Yip, that's right, per second.

Let me repeat that . . .

Three . . . Hundred . . . Thousand . . . Kilometers . . . In . . . One . . . Second.

In theory, if somebody struck a match in total darkness 300,000 km away in a straight line, you are supposed to see the light produced by the match in about the very same instant.

If we could speed up the Pioneer 10 space craft like this . . .

. . . we could reduce the 21 months to Jupiter to round and about an hour.

Let your mind race ahead.

Can you imagine our moon, approximately 384,400 km from earth?

At the speed of light, you can reach it in about 1.2 seconds.

Yesirree; you can be at the moon and back in 2.43 seconds flat.

Now that's pretty fast, isn't it?

Maybe I will finish my Jack, say . . . about the 257.733[th] time around?

Now the sun, 1,392,000 km in diameter, is 150,000,000 km (called an astronomical unit) from earth.

At 300,000 km per second sunlight took . . .

- *8 minutes to reach earth*

- *5 hours 30 min to reach Pluto, the most distant planet in our solar system and about 5,900,000,000 (5,900 million) km from the sun*

- *to reach the nearest star, Proxima Centauri in the Alfa Centauri constellation will take another 4.3 years*

All the while the planet we are on right now is traveling around the exact same sun, at 111,220 km (67,000 miles) per hour through space . . .

. . . And, spinning at a speed of 1,660 km (1 000 miles) per hour around its own axis.

You don't have to be a rocket scientist to know that the speed light travels in 365 days, or 1 year, is called a light-year.

You need more than a pocket calculator though, to determine:

- *That light travel in one light-year the distance of 9,460,800,000,000 km or 9.5 million, million (9.5 billion) kilometers*

- *Our own star system, the Milky Way, 85,000 light years (85,000 x 9,460,800,000,000 km) in diameter revolve around the sun as center point, at 800,000 km per hour once every 225 million years*

- *On a clear moonless night you can see from South Africa in the direction of the South Pole, two small constellations of stars that look for the naked eye like small clouds, called Magellan's clouds (named after the Portuguese seafarer Magellan).*

Both the constellations are outside our Milky Way.

The nearest one, about 170,000 light-years (170,000 x 9,460,800,000,000 km) from earth with a diameter of 22,000 light-years consists of about 10 milliard stars. The second one is about 205,000 light-years (205,000 x 9,460,800,000,000 km) from earth, 10,000 light-years in diameter and consists of 2 milliard stars

- *Andromeda, our closest neighboring 'Milky Way', with a diameter of 180,000 light-years (x 9,460,800,000,000 km) lays still another 2.3 million light-years (x 9,460,800,000,000 km) afar*

- *The closest star system we can observe is still more than 5,000 million light-years (x 9,460,800,000,000 km) further*

Some astronomers are off the opinion that this expansion started approximately 13.7 billion years ago . . .

. . . And . . . That's not the end!!

It's just the beginning!!

It is still expanding at astronomical rate . . . !!

That's absolutely amazing, isn't it?

But what is the point of all this?

My point is . . .

It is not that hard to realize, looking out the window of a modern-day luxury airliner at an altitude of a mere 10,000 meters at a mere 1,000 km/hour that people seemed to fade to . . . well . . .

NON-EXISTENCE?

What is the meaning of all this?

What I mean is this . . .

If there is a Divine Creator, GOD, way up there in *'Heaven'* at some couple o' trillion x 9,460,800,000,000 kilometer, and still expanding at astronomical rate, looking back would . . .

- *. . . take a mighty fine eye to establish where earth is, let alone where us humans are . . .* AND

- *. . . to know when 1 out of 90,000 to 140,000 hair on almost every individual person's head, of the 700 billion people on this planet, is lost.*

It seems, **to me at least**, like shooting arrows at random in the dark in the hope that you might hit the target.

Okay, let's get our feet back on the ground here for a moment.

Maybe I'm missing the basics here.

I suppose GOD is almighty and powerful enough to do anything.

Fair enough, I'm not questioning that.

But, isn't GOD also with-In us? Is it really possible for God to be both *In Heaven* as well as *In-Side* us; AND *In Between* . . . right?

SO . . . if you are only one person out of the minority of people that's been intrigued enough to read this far . . .

Congratulations!!

This is going to be one hell-of-a journey.

2.

a Simple Story . . .

*'I wish to live deliberately, to front only the essential facts of life
and see if I could learn what it had to teach, and not
when I come to die, discover that I had not lived.'*

~ Henry David Thoreau

IN 1958 A WHITE boy was born in a small little village of Somerset
East, Eastern Cape, South Africa.

Born as the only child to a father, a motor mechanic and his house-
wife mother, both at the time already in their late 30's, the chances
of having any children eluded them for more than 10 years.

Just like Hannah in The Bible (1 Sam 1:11) the little boy's mother
made a solemn pledge that if God gave her a child, she'd promise
to dedicate this child to God as long as she lives.

The little boy grew up unaware of his mother's promise in a stable,
lower to middle-class, Christian-family environment until the age
of 7.

Like most boys always do, the spirit of adventure was inevitably and one day he was playing 'camping out' in the backyard of their home.

In true South African tradition, camping out is associated with braai-vleis (barbecue), and soon enough he's got a nice little fire going and everything couldn't be better.

As could be expected, the wooden shelter underneath where the small fire was started, soon joined in the merriment of the occasion and wasn't it for the intervention of his father the situation could have been catastrophic.

That night the young boy couldn't sleep as he was tormented by the incident of that day.

Getting out of bed to peek out the window for the umpteenth time that night to established if the fire was really extinguished, desperate measures prevailed and as he lie exhausted in bed, started to pray silently.

He promised the Lord that if He can make him calm, he would dedicate his life to Him.

The young boy immediately fell into a deep sleep.

At that very same instant the young boy became a dedicated Christian.

At the age of 12, the boy's father passed away.

At the age of 17 the young man joined the South African law enforcement environment in 1975, amidst Nelson Mandela's

African National Congress' (ANC) struggle against the 'white apartheid' regime.

At the height of his career after nearly 20 years of dedicated service, the young man became part of a delegation to the political detainee's education in the province as well as implemented, at that time, a relative new concept of prisoners' community re-integration program into society.

As part of his duties to the pre-amble of the first South African open democratic election as well as towards the release of Nelson Mandela from prison in 1994, this young man and a fellow officer and personal friend, entered black 'shanty squatter townships' to verify addresses and the willingness of kinfolk to support parolees on probation.

As these two young men delicately tipsy-toed their way through one-lane dirt roads, potholes and corrugated shacks, sitting on the edge of their seats in an unmarked Volkswagen Golf 1.3*l*.

Clad in private clothes, without escort or armed support, they are trying and willing themselves to be as inconspicuous as hell, be quick about it and get the flip out of there as soon as they can.

As white people amidst a black suburbia, in a country of turmoil, unrest and 'necklace murders' (re: putting a motorcar tire around a living human and setting it on fire), as did happened to one of their colleagues only a couple of days earlier, the two young men felt like sticking out as sore eyes and could just as well been dancing on the rooftops in pink too-toe's and shouting their presence.

Rounding a corner they ran themselves into their greatest nightmare.

A big mass congregation of black people in black attire fill their entire field of vision.

Everywhere they looked in the street, in front of the car and next to the road, surrounded by a hoard of black people there was nowhere to go, nowhere to run.

No time for fear or a prayer.

Just an utterly silent acceptance and quiet awareness of their fate.

That was it. It was over.

Everything worked and lived for, a lifetime of good deeds and intentions disintegrated into nothingness.

AND . . . Nothing happened.

The worst case scenario turned out to be lots of young black kids in black uniform, coming out of the school grounds after school on their way home.

Safely back at home base, the two young men just sat there in utter silence in the car after switching of the engine, each with their own thoughts . . .

Finally braking silence the young man's colleague asked him just one question . . .

MARIUS asked **ME**;

'Do you think God was with us today?'

And for the first time in **MY** life I was stumbling to give a straight answer.

What if the situation had turned out for the worst?

I thought I was on top of things. I thought I knew the answer all my life. Or so it seems.

Wasn't this obvious? Shouldn't it be?

After all these years I was going down . . . *hard.*

In fact, I was *falling . . .*

Falling Higher

'I thought that I felt alright with my world,
Now, what I knew seems taken by someone,
Probing me, waiting if I take the bait,
Surrender, step into the line'

From the song 'Falling Higher' by Helloween ~
Deris; Andi; Weikath; Michael

3.

What's Happening

'It is the heart that makes a man rich. He is rich according to what he is, not what he has.'

Henry Ward Beecher

F OR NEARLY 20 YEARS after that incident I was stunned, falling and stumbling.

I felt as if I was alone in a desert and everything about my life was going down the drain.

All the answers I thought I had didn't satisfied me any longer and I rebelled against what I have always felt so sure of before.

I was looking at myself and it was some-one else I see.

There was some-one inside my head that wasn't me.

It seemed like an enormous risk to challenge and examined my belief systems and it took a good measure of courage to begin such questioning.

Because when we are courageous enough to give serious attention to such uncertain feelings emerging in our souls we can feel unsure as to whom we are, what our purpose in the world are and how our life makes any sense at all.

It was this very risk of feeling so unsettled that kept me from ever challenging the faith of my childhood.

No honest mind can exclude doubt, ignore criticism or shut its ears against reason.

If we could do these things we should be left, not with faith, but with a head-in-the-sand superstition.

Never imagine that faith can ever be furthered by suppressing honest doubt, let alone by suppressing evidence.

All truth is One, and religion must be as eager as science to know the truth as far as man can perceive it.

If something I have treasured as truth is really contradicted by unanswerable evidence, then in the name of the God of Truth I must part with it however venerable it may be.

Stepping outside of what I knew in order to glimpse what I do not know does not necessarily lead to a point of forsaking my religious convictions.

The moment I was willing to go deep down within and challenge what I have known and believed, I found in the swirl of chaos the God beyond all conceptions.

Once I overcome my fear of encountering that chaos, I found what my heart longed for, what my mind can only barely grasp, what my soul only dimly imagined.

Questioning is not the enemy of faith.

It is the growing edge of faith.

Stepping out was a sign that I am in search for God-Self.

It became thought in action.

My soul was longing to know without any pretence, without easy answers, without the superficiality to which religious systems fall prey.

It was not an easy journey.

In fact, it was a tumultuous odyssey in surprising and unexpected ways.

Since I challenged the belief systems I have grown up with, it has merely becomes a springboard for my soul in searching for the pearl of great price.

It is the freedom to be independent.

Not by birth or by law, but by choice.

It is the courage to stand up when the rest is sitting down . . .

. . . The powerful realization that I finally stand for something, and not fall for anything.

If you are one of those people *craving* to connect with *God*, your *Soul*, your *Creator* or whatever else you may choose to call your *One True Source*, and you have this *desire*, a spiritual *longing* to liberate yourself from the shackles of everyday norm, this is for you.

It is our birth-right and if you don't have it right now, you must reclaim it.

God will honour your search and love you through the journey.

So why is it that so many 'normal' people continue to line themselves up for practically what is to be considered mental suicide?

We have been conditioned to allow all sorts of mental programming to affect our lives without even being aware of the damage which this does to our mental state.

To a much larger extent than people would like to admit, our beliefs create, control and affect our entire reality.

Some people will even kill and die for their beliefs.

Our understanding of what is 'objective' truth is that we all agree on something—the sky is blue, the rock is brown, the grass is green.

And yet it turns out that the reality out there—the sky, the rock, the grass—can only be internalized by means of our perceptions.

This means our brain takes the information our senses provide and turn that into an impression, something that registers, something we are aware of.

We take in masses of information all the time we are awake.

But if the brain does not 'inform' us that it is there, we won't 'see' anything—we will not be aware that we are looking at something.

Of all the masses of information we take in, the brain chooses what it considers relevant to us and saves us the bother of examining every leaf on a tree, every blade of grass.

So it screens out what seems irrelevant—or what it cannot make sense of—or what it does not expect to see.

In the same way we do not consciously think of how to tie our shoelaces or walk, saves us a lot of time and energy.

The problem comes in when we find it has made sure we see what we expect to see and so we miss the TRUTH or what we need to see.

We can never create Truth.

We can only discover and uses it.

And, so, for the first time in my life I was challenging my believe systems.

I have found that once I start doing this, everything I am, everything I do and have done came together in a new pattern that is completely different from before.

I discovered that I lost my religion, but indeed not my faith.

It can only be that way when everything involved me, from my head to my toes and beyond—to my cells, to the molecules that make up the cells, the DNA and the genes and down to the atoms that make up the molecules and to the sub-atomic particles, the protons, neutrons and the electrons.

I was living according to a preconceived notion of what my life was supposed to be.

Only to realize I was starving mentally, emotionally and spiritually.

And I was starving for life.

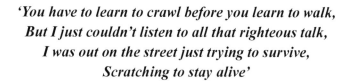

'You have to learn to crawl before you learn to walk,
But I just couldn't listen to all that righteous talk,
I was out on the street just trying to survive,
Scratching to stay alive'

From the song 'Amazing' by Aerosmith ~
Steven; Joe; Brad; Tom; Joey

4.

$$\mathcal{W}hat's\ \mathcal{L}ife$$

'There are some things so dear, some things so precious, some things so eternally true, that they are worth dying for. And I submit to you that if a man has not discovered something that he will die for, he isn't fit to live.'

Martin Luther King ~ Detroit, USA Jun 23, 1963

IMAGINE CREATION ALL BEING started with only a crude chisel and a flat piece of rock.

Way, way BC (Before Computers).

Seven days to create a world is very limited, no matter how you structure your day-light savings time.

There was definitely a lot of things to comprehend in those hectic days.

Whatever you call it, every little thing needed a sequence . . .

- Rain: Ocean—evaporation-condensation-precipitation-rain

- Butterflies: Caterpillar-pupa-chrysalis-butterfly

- Petrol: Dinosaurs-fossilization-Arabs drilling-$500 a barrel-petrol

- Avocados: Fruit falls to the ground, oops-umm-huh . . . ?

During my experience working in the bee-keeping industry, it was perfectly clear to me that bees almost beat us on the evolutionary ladder.

They are very clever indeed, I mean, there is no other being alive on this planet making that natural, sweet, unpreserved stuff out of almost nothing, from clover, orange blossom to buckwheat, just so we can pour it all over our waffles and toast.

These are the creatures responsible for the propagation of various species of flora in the world.

Granted, that is a very good point, even if I say so myself.

But how on earth would bees stick the matches in the pip of an avocado pear for science class.

How would bees find a nice size jam jar to put the pip in and how would they carry it from the faucet without spilling?

Indeed, sticking the matches in would present some serious challenges if they could not get the box open?

But, hence the wisdom in generations of western education is that the human factor is essential in the cycle of life.

So . . . the Creator's chisel flow through it all.

It must have been clear then, however, it will take another creature to ensure the survival of avocado's everywhere.

It would have to be build stronger, faster and intelligent enough to select an appropriate size vessel, with eyes facing forward not to trip while carrying it.

Most of all it would need opposable thumbs.

But instead of us human beings using our thumbs to reforest the earth, we use them to teach bees their place, shove smoke in their houses and steal their lunch.

So, here we got stuck with this species on the planet commonly known as homo-sapiens.

They are heavily influenced by the fact that for them there is a beginning and an end—a time to be born and a time to die.

This probably might explain their time-dependent behavior between each other.

Impatience, intolerance, anxiety, stress, frustration with life and them-selves and a desire for a realm beyond death which they called 'Heaven'.

Yet they cannot adequately describe it.

We find individuals, families and nations bickering, fighting and killing one another for material goods, riches and power so they can, what they perceive, live in relative peace and comfort.

Little ones are forced to grow up quickly just to keep up with all the new information thrown their way.

The older of their species are not given any time at all.

There once was a bushy haired fellow with an inquisitive mind— called Einstein, investigated this concept of atoms and stuff as well as the realm of time.

He came up with interesting perspectives.

But no-one completely understands his theories.

Then there are some particular pieces of literature a lot of humans in certain societies adhered to in their lives.

These are called such as The Bible, The Qur'an, Torah, Sutra, Talmud or what-ever, and are generally accepted as revelations from their Divine Master explaining why humans are acting the way they do, and should do.

Yet most of them are oblivious to it.

Instead, many of them have created many purposes and religions in life.

Each of their members being told that they are the chosen ones; that every-one of them is the center-piece of a master plan.

Yet nothing ever satisfies the majority of them.

After closer observation though, there are still some that do want to understand the deeper meaning of our existence.

These people want *Reason to Believe.*

Not the reason *'Why'* to believe.

But to Think, to Reason, to Grasp and Understand with their *MINDS* great design and purpose in the natural and spiritual world around them.

To them has been given *a Spirit* to comprehend the existence of physical life.

As they begin to understand, their whole concept of time and purpose changes.

Now, I will be the first one to admit that my possible answer to the mystery of humankind as I see it, will not find favor with everyone.

Especially, much less from a guy desperately trying to find himself in life, sitting on a barstool in the corner of a pub, frantically taking down notes on a napkin while trying to attract the barman's attention for another Jack Daniels.

5.

. . . the Story Continues

> *'I'd rather be a HAS-BEEN*
> *Than a MIGHT-HAVE-BEEN by far*
> *For a might-have-been has NEVER-BEEN*
> *But a HAS-BEEN was once an ARE'*

> *Milton Berle*

SINCE MY BACHELOR IN Theology Studies it was always a dream for me to write and publish the title *FALLING HIGHER*, either in book form or on the internet as a web-site, or both.

But I never took the opportunity and the time to actually do it.

It was always a dormant, constant awareness; looking for opportunities to broaden and improves my horizons in this field.

After extensively working in the United States of America, I seriously took this opportunity.

I published both this book as well as registered the website *www. fallinghigher.com*

The fact that you are reading this book shows that you too would like to . . .

- maximize your God-given potential

- give definition to your choices

- get outside the problem and see around the situation

- wrap your spirit as a catalyst in God's sovereignty and into God-given success

Did you know?

- The simple act of just reading these sentences involved millions of impulses firing across billions of synapsis in your body

- Your heart goes about its business circulating five quarts of blood through a hundred thousand miles of veins, arteries and capillaries

Normally we focused so much on *what we are doing* or *where we are going.*

But our primary concern should rather be *who we are becoming* in the process.

Too often we let how we're going to do it get in the way of how God is going to do it.

Our God-given ability has much more to do with *being* than *doing.*

I know it is not easy.

It's *not* about being in the right place at the right time.

It is about being the *right person—even* in the wrong circumstances.

To choose successfully is not circumstantial.

It do not depend on the primary significance based on information which suggests that something is true but does not prove that it is true.

The danger lies in getting stuck in neutral.

It is astonishing how great and wonderful things tend to happen to us if we keep our minds open expectantly all the time.

Always think of the best, never of the worst.

If the worst invades our thoughts, consciously think in terms of how to make it the best.

Everybody wants to be successful.

How successful we are, has nothing to do with how resourceful or clever we are.

It has everything to do with *maximizing* our God-given *'giftedness'*.

Very few will spell it out right.

How will we know if we achieved anything if we don't spell it out for ourselves?

We might achieve our goals only to realize at the end of our days that they shouldn't be our goals in the first place.

gation">FALLING HIGHER

It's so easy being busy climbing the ladder of success that we fail to realize that the ladder is not leaning against anything.

Sometimes the chances are possible we will succeed at nothing or at the wrong thing, because we climb the wrong ladder.

I come to realize that to make a living and acquire money and material things is *'small change'* to the challenges, the purpose to live your *'dream'*, the reason for being.

For sure, to be in modern life is to earn wealth.

Everybody needs money.

Money makes the world go round, right?

So does five shots of tequila, what's the point?

But to work only for the sake of making money is like playing football with your eyes on the scoreboard instead of the ball.

You *will* lose the game . . . !!

The journey will choose us, but the adventure is ours to choose.

In less than 10 years, I have experienced more than I did in a lifetime of 45 years before that.

I've experienced the world:-

- *I flew over the Sahara Desert in North Africa; the Eiffel Tower in Paris, France; over volcanic smoke at the*

33

Icelandic outskirts of the North Pole; as well as been to Amsterdam, London and Dubai and more . . .

- *I have been to the most Southern tip of Africa, the official meeting place of two of the world's mighty oceans, the Indian and the Atlantic, an important geographical point indicating both the beginning and the end of Africa; and did a 4x4 course and trails in an owner-driven Land Rover Defender in South Africa*

- *I visited the first, original Ripley's believe-it-or-not museum and took a helicopter flip over St Augustine; been to the Walt Disney Theme Parks in Orlando; the Kennedy Space Centre at Cape Canaveral; and survived the 2004 hurricanes Charley, Frances, Ivan and Jeanne in Florida, USA*

- *I have walked 4.6 miles, 175 feet beneath the mountain in Carlsbad National Caverns; visited the Roswell Alien Museum; eat jalapenos, drink tequila and slept in front of a fire in a log cabin in an Apache reservation of the Sacramento Mountain's Lincoln Forestry, New Mexico*

- *I took a rollercoaster ride at Six Flags, Dallas; ate a chimi-changa with coffee in Muleshoe; and saw a musical drama in Palo Duro, Texas the second biggest canyon in the USA*

- *I operated an oversized, class A commercial driver's license, with 18-wheeler semi-trucks over the interstates of 41 American States; visited Mt Rushmore in the Black Hills, SD; Times Square, NY; Jack Daniels Distillers, TN; drank a skull crusher cocktail at the oldest Pirate House in Tybee Island, GA; and saw a genuine western rodeo in the hometown of the infamous western writer, Louis L'Amour in Jamestown, ND*

•   *. . . and then some many, many more . . .*

But what is the point?

Thousands of people have done that—and even so much more than I did.

The point is. . . It is not about me; It is about *YOU*, and what *YOU* can become in *YOUR* life!!

We need to get to know ourselves, find and reconnect with humanity again.

The ability to choose is one of the great gifts God has given every human being.

What we do with it, is our gift back to God.

And to choose wisely is to know the pleasures of God's freedom.

Although our consciousness is tightly leashed when it comes to literally creative abilities and, if we could easily manipulate reality with pure conscious intent, the world would be in utter chaos.

But ultimately I believe that our consciousness does have that capability.

When we do, we will see, by dropping inflated and unrealistic expectations, we are able to achieve incredible things, using our *God-given* ingredients to set ourselves free in *Mind, Body and Spirit.*

FALLING HIGHER is all about that.

This means we can learn to choose the role our Spiritual Nature manifested in the concrete, material world all the time . . .

. . . And, what reality is by understanding and willingly taking responsibility for our own minds.

There is only one condition.

I found that, once I started this fire, I couldn't let go of the flame.

It became impossible to return to my old life.

It became a living, breathing part of my whole being.

I was born again.

'Shade my eyes to all that's around me,
Except that star I've needed to reach,
Too late, my fate now surrounds me
For all I've gained, I couldn't keep'

From the song 'Without Your Love' by Whitecross ~
Scott; Rex; Mike; Scott

6.

The Formula

> 'My religion consists of a humble admiration of the illimitable
> Superior Spirit, Who reveals It-Self in the slight details we are
> able to perceive with our frail and feeble mind, and the deeply
> emotional conviction of the presence of a Superior Reasoning
> Power which is revealed in the incomprehensible universe.'
>
> *Albert Einstein*

F OR ME THE PROBLEM to the answer is in the Power Formula
I have personally designed myself as a launch-pad for a
meaningful and rewarding life.

The Falling Higher Formula ™

$$ \$ = M \left(\sqrt[4]{E^{tf} U^{pi}} \right) L $$

I believe this is what the Power of the Universe, God, really intend
for us.

I believe that the Omnipotent Divine God wants us to make the
most of our own potential and to do what we need, to know
ourselves.

Each and every one of us has been given all we need to create meaningful, positive, rewarding lives.

And that it is our responsibility to fulfil this mission on earth.

We are not fated to live a certain life.

We are all sparks of God.

We experiencing our creativity in the mental reality which enables us to live physically in the material world.

All the processes that keep us alive are about the nature of electro-chemical energy imprinted in our subconscious mind and bodies.

This includes the way thoughts, ideas and decisions travel from the mind along our nerves to our muscles and organs, affecting and directing our actions.

The universe is a vast, inseparable web of dynamic activity.

Everything in the universe is made up of vibrations of energy.

At its most primary level, the universe seems to be whole and undifferentiated, a fathomless sea of energy that permeates every object and every act.

Everything in the universe affects everything else.

It is all One and we all are but part of this One giant whole.

All of God is present at any and every point within it.

God in all and through all.

The Power whose centre is everywhere and circumference is nowhere.

God is not approaching a point nor receding from it.

God Is always at it.

Figure 1: God as the centre of faith, with all non-believers outside God's circumference.

Figure 2: God in all and through all, whose centre is everywhere, whose circumference is nowhere and who is always at any and every point in it.

Not only is the universe alive and constantly changing, but our thoughts, too, are vibrations of energy.

Our thoughts being energy, it only makes sense that our repeated vibrating within the larger web of reality would have an effect upon that reality.

And the way to do this is to find out what we have *with-In* us and uses it well.

Talk, live, act, believe and know that you are a center in the One.

God does not need to micro-engineer or micro-manage the evolution of life forms, on earth, or for that matter, anywhere . . .

- *God IS the intelligent design, basic laws of physics and the associated physical constants*

- *God IS the creator, the ONE which give life to matter; the POWER that holds the atoms together that they may produce form.*

We do not know what the future holds, but we can know what holds the future.

I believe that this principle are built into every human being.

Each of us is packed full of this potential by the ONE presence in all of us.

We stand on the edge of consciousness in finding that missing link.

The link is a natural phenomenon that teaches and justifies a principle of logic and non-judgmental reasoning.

This principle is justified by what contemporary physics demonstrates as a scientific fact.

Combining this reasoning with our current process expands our consciousness of reality.

In this enlightened consciousness we are personally empowered to resolve all problems and live the good life as from the beginning God had meant us to live it.

'Well people look and people stare, well
I don't think that I even care
you work your life away and what do they give?
You're only killing yourself to live'

From the song 'Killing your-self to Live' by Black Sabbath ~
Ozzy; Geezer; Tony; Bill

7.

Burn Out

S O HERE I WAS on a highway to the danger zone.

From the age of 7, I was always this *'example'* of what a
Christian should be in life.

Always being considerate to the need of others; always putting
other people first . . .

One of the passions my dad had was rugby (football).

He was a pretty good player himself in his younger days, and a
life-long enthusiast until his death.

As for myself, I must have been quite a bit of a failure to him in
this regard; it just was not for me.

I am not much of a ball person.

44

Just before my dad pass away, he must have realized this.

Before my first year of high school he bought me a bicycle; which incidentally became the passion of my life.

My own set of wheels!!

I became mobile.

I took up competitive cycling as an outdoor activity in those early days.

It should have been clear to me then, it was a signal that I was disengaging myself from something that was constantly calling me for experiences my soul wanted to have in this life.

My soul was yelling at me to go in a different direction, but I was not listening to my Inner Voice.

In my heart of hearts, I wanted to be somebody else.

But I was not listening.

The day I won my first cycling race, I could not believe it.

As a young Christian, winning was not my first goal in life.

Competitiveness was just not my style.

As I crossed the line in first place that day, I looked back and was pretty amazed at this feat I had achieved.

But I had this feeling, knawing away at my soul, the feeling that, somehow, this was not right.

I even felt bad for my fellow competitors for not winning.

When I finished high school I started to work right away . . . and keep at the same institution for 21 years.

Everyday stress is a factor that we are all contend with and suitably managed to a point that, despite the anxieties experienced, we come out the other side proud of our accomplishments or perseverance to succeed.

There is nothing wrong with healthy pressure and motive to keep us on our toes.

Without goals or deadlines nothing would ever get done and no forward movement would be made.

But after a stay in the same business for 21 years, and when I left, getting reimbursed as part of my severance package the total of 360 days accumulative paid leave, it was a sure sign of serious trouble.

To be exact, what it all boiled down to is this.

Out of 21 years dedicated service, I did not took my allowed annual paid leave of 30 days per year, for 12 years—over half of my career.

The outcome was certain—Chaos.

This was reflected in my everyday life as objections and excuses to better myself.

At the deepest level, where the boundaries between physical and spiritual being are no longer clear (the sub-atomic quantum level), it contaminated my mind, body and spirit.

And the world around me!

It felt as if I was forever trying to find method in madness.

It infuriated me that the more I wanted to know, the less I understand.

It was when such demands become unmanageable and overwhelming that I lost sight of the light at the end of the tunnel and got consumed by a crushing sense of lost control.

I did not realized I was deep-freezed.

I was trying to break down doors I shouldn't go through.

I failed miserably by trying to figure out how to do it, instead of how God is going to do it.

So I actually end up doing nothing at all.

One fact ring true; wrongness can never produce rightness and vice versa.

Two negatives cannot make a positive.

Finding oneself in high pressure zones during the day is an unavoidable element we all need to learn to handle.

Provided we are trying to achieve any sense of advancement, the more we take on, so the pressure mounts.

I found myself more and more moving the boundaries to the outer limits.

I was pretty messed up, trying to leave but could not find the door.

Everybody told me to relax and not to stress too much.

The more people telling me that, the more I can't stand listening to it.

It drove me up the wall!!

Pray the blood of Jesus over it, my pharmacist advised me.

I could not listen to all that righteous talk anymore.

I needed something *'real'*, real bad.

My doctor prescribed me medication, and after three sessions at a psychiatrist I knew that both of them was not going to work for me either.

After all, what was going to happen, was that I still wanted to end it all.

But with all those medication, it would just still my mind and I won't feel bad when I did it anyway.

There *had* to be something else.

I was scratching to stay alive.

I desperately needed a helping hand far more than lips that pray.

I needed to gain that healthy driving force that keep the cogs turning.

I was living from minute to minute, hour by hour, day by day.

One thing that kept my head above water, was a phrase I read in a Readers Digest article once before . . .

'I'm still here, I've made it this far'.

And I keep repeating it to myself over and over and over again.

Until that one fateful day . . . !!

A senior officer, and I will always remember that moment, pulled me into her office and become the only person putting the finger exactly on my problem.

Listening intently as I spill my guts, she slowly proceeded with opening a drawer on her desk, and as I speak, silently hand me a torn out magazine article.

And for the first time, as I looked at it, a feeble, tiny, minute, small little light start seeping through . . .

It dimly dawned on me . . .

If you find yourself in a hole, *STOP DIGGING!!*

The cover photo in that magazine article said it all.

It was a hand holding a candle, *burning on both sides.*

The name of the article ~ 'Burn-Out'.

> *'The American psychoanalyst Dr Herbert J. Freudenberger*
> *coined the term 'Burn-Out' in 1972, and is NOT the same as*
> *depressed, overworked or mentally broken down. It is a subtle*
> *process, in which somebody is gradually caught in a state of*
> *mental fatigue, completely empty and drained of all energy.'*
>
> *(Cherniss, 1980, in Schaufeli & Buunk, 1992)*

I can barely try to describe this over-arching phenomena of 'Burn-Out' the same way as the simplified version of a single, 4 stroke motorcar engine.

Risqué slang among automotive enthusiasts based the typical 4 stroke method used in almost all internal combustion engines of the cars of our times today, respectively the 'suck', 'squeeze', 'bang' and 'blow' principle ~

1. Intake stroke ~
   The piston descends from top dead center increasing the volume of the cylinder while a mixture of air and fuel is *sucked* into the cylinder through the intake port.

2. Compression stroke ~
   The piston returns to the top of the cylinder *squeezes* or compressing the air-fuel mixture into the cylinder head.

3. Power stroke ~
    The compressed air-fuel mixture is ignited, resulting in the compressed air-fuel mixture to *explode* and forces the piston back down.

4. Exhaust stroke ~
    The piston once again returns to top dead center and *expels* the spent fuel-air mixture through the exhaust valve.

The moral of the story . . .

Although there is only one engine operating the car, it cannot properly function as a unit if we alienate any of its mechanical components and principles.

An adequate description of Burn-Out is like . . .

. . . the 'suck, squeeze, bang and blow' of an 8 cylinder motorcar engine, operating only on 1 piston, at 3000 revolutions per minute, doing 100 miles per hour in 1st gear . . .

. . . and see how long it can keep up.

Now take this kind of pressure, amplify it by a thousand and sprinkle it with extra lack of interest, enthusiasm and indifference, mix in some cynicism, contempt and selfishness, leave out any hint of motivation and you have yourself a crispy, toasted burn-out.

We have approximately 60,000 separate and often disconnected thoughts during the day.

Being too hard on ourselves, it is very difficult to focus on a consistent basis on what we want to achieve.

There is an enormous difference between regular stress, everyday pressures and that of a full scale, systems shut down.

Burn-out occurs when energy, involvement and effectivity erode into fatigue, cynicism and an inability to function productively.

Burn-out is generally long-term exhaustion and diminished interest in life.

Not only do it differ from person to person, if left untreated it create a powerful downward spiral begetting and feeding off each other.

As burnout is a long term, gradual process, it unfortunately also cannot be cured overnight.

Recovering from burnout is a process that is almost as long as the downward spiral causing it.

But . . . Is it ultimately possible to find meaning in Burn-Out?

Yebo *yes,* it *is* possible.

I'm the living proof of that!!

What I am trying to illustrate here is, that when life leaves you feeling bleak about every aspect encompassing your life, this is when you need to pay attention to yourself.

This is when things may become a problem.

By this I don't mean to suggest that you are scheduled for a meltdown from having a series of bad days.

With the very nature of the career growth *'disease'*, there are ways in which to avoid such catastrophic results and maintain a bountiful career and life balance.

Prevention is better than cure.

We have to shift the intensity from something so colossal that you cannot see past the multitude of hurdles you are expected to defeat, to that of something being unpleasantly manageable.

Most of the people can, and do just that.

But instead of providing you with an airy-fairy means of achieving a sense of Nirvana, to achieve this precious balance, I can only present you with a sense of life-confirming principles as outlined in my *Falling Higher Power Formula*™

I have found in my life, the way the *Falling Higher Formula*™ can be utilized.

It is an integral part of our existence!!

Most information we received is 'noise'.

And it becomes impossible to tell whether, buried within the crackle of static, if it is a genuine message or signal.

Ignore day to day information overload and tune in less frequently.

Clutter. Distraction. Confusion.

Tune out as much of this kind of noise as you can.

Not only does it waste our time, but it confuses and misleads us.

What happens if we don't? Do we fall off the planet?

Something is actually just eating up our time without doing us any good.

Keep an eye out for how it creeps back into our life, pretending to be something important.

These are attitudes and beliefs that are firmly entrenched in many people's minds.

Whether we are right or wrong is sometimes a matter of religious belief.

We have to remove the barriers so that us ordinary people can free ourselves from slavery and enjoy a rich and rewarding life in every area.

More and more people are learning this than ever before in their lives!

Love that kind of open-mindedness . . .

Listen to that quiet little inner voice that says; 'Even though you don't understand, there is something of value to learn here'.

So just keep going. Keep stumbling forward. Never surrender to the false.

Embrace the confusion. Love it, because it means we're growing.

It's proof, in fact!

The really important things will find their way to us anyway.

We can't expect to understand everything straight away, and stretching our minds to a new level is not only good for our growth, but it also helps us reach new levels of achievement in every area of life!

The long and the short of it is, we will get the results we expect.

Often when everything goes wrong with us, it simply is because we are wrong ourselves.

We are our own worst enemies.

When we act wrong, think wrong and been motivated by a wrong psychology, we cannot expect wonderful things happening to us.

When we become right with-In, we will find ourselves turning on miracles.

I think that if we choose 'big' for the right reasons, God will bless 'big'.

That certainly doesn't mean we can play God like a slot machine.

When we choose a life of obedience to the call, we position ourselves for blessings.

Take your foot of the accelerator.

Be still, be humble.

Stay hungry.

'You tell me what I should do, you want to take control,
You try to reach me inside, and change the way I think,
It seems to me you want to rule all over me,
Why don't you practice what you preach and let me be.'

From the song 'If my mind is evil' by White Lion ~
Mike; Vito; Greg; James

8.

Falling Higher

'Anything we do not examine, we do not truly know or appreciate.
We have no idea how brainwashed we are. Meanwhile,
tapping us on the shoulder is the true value, the true gold,
the gold we do not recognize. The Gold of the Truth.

Hannes Dreyer

I T ALL STARTED WITH a small packet of sugar.

One day is was sitting in an Italian pizza and pasta restaurant in the Western Cape, South Africa.

It was just a couple of days away before I had to leave for the United States of America, waiting on my wife, who ran some errands, to join me.

At the table where I sat, was the usual container holding all the necessary items you normally found in restaurants like ketchup, salt and pepper, etc.

Also in the holder was this sugar sachets, eloquently inscribed on the back with some inspirational thoughts.

As I idle leafed through them, I randomly selected a packet out of the bunch.

And my life changed forever.

The inscription on the one I selected read as follows . . .

'Believe as though you are, and you will be'

~ Ernest Holmes

After a long series of events ranging well over a period of 20 years, dealing with life from started my own business, divorce, being a single parent for two teenage daughters right through to the death of a once in a lifetime best friend anybody can ever wished for, for the very first time everything really started to open up.

Like I said, I do not claim that I have the final answers in life.

But maybe, just maybe, I can help just one desperate soul gain some meaning in this life.

Here's the liberating reality . . .

To play it safe is to lose the game.

We miss 100% of the shots we do not take.

Success is living with authentic integrity.

When we lose sight of our God ordained goals, subjugated to our temporal responsibilities, we pawn our God-given *'dream'* for living the *'American dream'*.

Reminds me of a man who comes to God and ask . . .

God, how long is a million years to you?
Well, God said, it's about a second.
Again the man asked; and how much is a million dollar worth
to you?
Well, God said, it's about a penny.
The man smiled and said; can I have a penny then.
For sure, God said, just give me a second.

For me it is rather an objective body of knowledge to sustain a personal faith that can deepen, transform and affirm the way many of us are today.

We need more backbone and less wishbone.

I am of the opinion that most, if not all Christians today had become rocking horse people with kaleidoscope eyes.

It gives them a lot to do, but they are not going anywhere.

They have reached a state of unfoldment, where a broader scope is possible.

The God of truth is not a God of fable.

There is but One Mind in the universe and all inquiry into Truth is an inquiry into this Mind.

Compared with the standard that God has set up, man's opinion is like a feather in the scale.

Since we know we did not create the creation ourselves, yet we and the creation do exist, it is logical to believe that some Eternal Cause created it.

It is, therefore, according to me, absolutely irresponsible for so many sincere thinking people, calling on their revealed religions, to reject and close their minds.

Christianity cannot just keep their corner of the world in abject ignorance, doing the same wherever their dim thoughts been propagated, and burden humanity in its advance nor drag it into the mire of ignorance and nullify all forward thought.

You see this is the whole secret.

The secret is . . .

There is no secret!!

If you are 150 trillion some odd light years away from earth and or beyond, or inside the human body at super micron cellular level, all our entire existence, this world and the total universe is, is Quantum Physics.

Think about it, it's as simple as that.

Quantum physics tells us that everything is energy.

It is pure *Chemical-Magnetic Energy.*

That is the way the universe is wired.

On a quantum level there is no time; time does not exist.

In quantum physics there is always both + and—charges.

All we have to learn is to flow our chemical-magnetic energy differently, for nothing affects our physical experience except how we vibrating our energy.

We create our own lives every minute every moment of the day.

The trick is to use only positive energy.

This can only happen if we truly align our energy with the Power of the Universe, GOD, and consciously feel connected to all Its potential—Every day of our lives.

Maybe that's what Jesus' teachings was all about?

In my opinion, the unseen Power of the Mind that comes through alignment with the Powerful Forces created in the universe is by far our most important tool.

We could call this taking spiritual responsibility!?

The infinity of wisdom is to follow the real method, whereby we may have the Power and the Inspiration of the Omnipotent Universal Mind, GOD, on demand at any time.

Doesn't this meant the *Kingdom of Heaven* is with-In us?

Our mission on earth should thus be a perfect understanding of the principles, forces, methods and combinations of Mind and our relationship to the Universal Mind.

That is what the Falling Higher Formula™ is all about!!

The Falling Higher Formula ™

$$\$ = M \left(\sqrt[4]{E^{t/}\,U^{pi}} \right) L$$

$\$ = GOD$ *[Spirit/Soul]*
M & L = Mind & Logos
A = Attitude
E = Emotions—Thoughts & Feelings
U = Understanding—Perceptions & Ignorance

Everything in the conscious universe consists of the ultra-fine line of unification between the Omnipresent Universal Intelligence— *God*—or *Spirit/Soul* . . .

. . . And the Power of the *Mind* and Source of *Logos*—logical reasoning and intelligence.

Let me simplify this by demonstrating it differently . . .

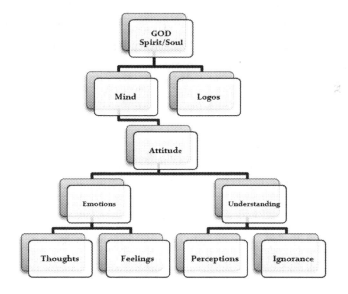

All the elements go down and affect the very particles of our being at a quantum / spiritual level!

It is the Universal Law, it is as simple as that.

Whether we plan it that way, or want it that way, or not.

It simply IS.

I believe once we awaken to this truth, once we become aware of this remarkable fact it becomes crystal clear that we can ultimately reach the highest level possible that Jesus was trying to tell us, the Kingdom of Heaven, or GOD.

And we can either be the master or the victim.

This means we have a great opportunity here to get rid of the self-imposed barriers in our own lives!

Since the world's injustices are not going to be solved by more injustices in the belief that the end will justify the means, I realize that the solution begins within me.

In other words, I take responsibility for my own mind and my own life.

All people are fortunate in having the most powerful tool already honed and operating, but they are not applying it correctly to their ends.

The 'suck, squeeze, bang and blow' Power of the Mind principle turns in perfect harmony, but it is not connected to the wheels.

No forward motion results.

There is no point being on the right track, but keep stationary all the time.

The Falling Higher Power Formula™ supports the point that without the active principle—the doing—a great idea is not going to get you anywhere.

To avoid this trap, visualize this entire method over and over again, so that you may use it whenever occasion requires.

For some reason, what has been known for many years about the creative Power of the Mind, is still not common knowledge.

This is the position most people are in today.

It is still dismissed as *wacky* or *new age* and therefore *silly* or *satanic*, or both.

Along with the grind of an unfulfilling job and the weight of responsibility, everyone wants an escape sometimes; and you should have one.

But we deny ourselves, we are supposed to *be grown up, take life seriously* and take *mental leaps* based on sloppy and wishful thinking.

Our minds become a Trojan horse on which unscrupulous powers will ride straight into our brains and our decision-making.

This is not surprising when you think about it, because the facts are usually rather unimpressive.

Where-as the ability to influence people through their minds is extremely impressive.

Especially, as most people haven't the faintest idea that their 'mental being' are used against their own better interests.

Our minds is so polarized, so *confokulated*, because we are pressing the same button over and over again.

It's the solution to it all, the one constant clawing for air beneath the mudslide of self-seeking and human foolishness.

I think that in the quest for higher truth, this could very well be the highest truth of it all.

As wonderful as all the hymns, the sermons, the church plays, theological studies and analyses are, the most mistrusted, startling truth in all of human history gets driven over.

It is the Mystery of mysteries, the Reality of realities.

It is this most cherished mystery, most precious reality crying out for its due.

Crying over its abandonment by man.

Heartbreak of heartbreaks, here we are and we missed it.

We opted for stubborn pride despite the obvious, and we missed it.

And missed it. And we kept right on missing it!!

The Power of the Mind and Source of Logos, that could expand our consciousness, surfaces quite clearly in the Bible . . .

- *'If you remain constant to my Word(*) you will find out the truth and the truth will set you free' [* Word, or Will of God ~ the English translation of the Greek term Logos which refers to the logic or reasoning of God]*

- *'I ask you by the mercy of God, to offer yourself as a living and Holy sacrifice acceptable to God for this is your rational worship dedicated to His service, but do not be conformed to the standards of this world but let God transform you inwardly by a complete renewal of your MIND'*

- *'Love God with all your heart, soul, strength and entire MIND, and love your neighbour as yourself, and you are not far from the Kingdom of God'*

- *'Because they (we) do not see, hear nor understand . . . ; for who-ever has, shall be given and they shall have in abundance, but who-ever has not, even what they have shall be taken away from them.*

  But rather seek the Kingdom of God and all these things shall be added unto you.

  In them the prophecy of Isaiah (6: 9-10) is full-filled which says, 'You shall hear and see without understanding (perceiving) for the MINDS of this people are dull (has grown fat), and they have heard heavily with their ears (they have stopped ears), and they have closed their eyes (as asleep) otherwise their MINDS would understand and should be converted and they will be healed.'

(John 8:31-32 / Mark 12:28-34 / Rom 12:2 / Matt 13: 1-58 / Mark 4:1-33 / Luke 8:4-15 / Luke 12:31)

This reasoning emphasis Jesus' oral or logos/logic teachings so that it should be fulfilled which was spoken through the prophet saying . . .

'I will utter things hidden from the world's foundation'.

The main point is always a ringing endorsement of figurative, spiritual principles.

This elevate our reasoning mind to that of the Reasoning/Will of God.

In this renewed *Mind*, our reasoning supports spiritual values.

We elevate our reasoning *Mind* to the same level as our spiritual thoughts and thus harmonizes our reasoning with our Spirit.

We will be born again mentally and spiritually.

For just as *Mind* and *Spirit* seek the same ends, it's the key to higher consciousness and doing *'on earth as it is in heaven',* as Jesus said we could, will no longer be an idealistic goal.

It will be a practical reality.

Our reference to God demands that we do this, lest we ascribe to God what is not His.

Our duty to ourselves demands it, lest we take fable for fact and rest our hope of salvation on a false foundation of sand.

Something more, therefore, is necessary than mere cry and wholesale assertion.

That something is TRUTH.

In order to arrive at truth, inquiry therefore is necessary.

As inquiry is the road to truth, he that is opposed to inquiry is not a friend to the truth.

But inquiry must have an honest principle to proceed on, some standard to be judged by and superior to human authority.

The presumption that the answer is revealed and then not be supported by seeking evidence, is a sure way to lead civilization down the blind alley of arrogant egotism and institutionalized error.

Clearly, Christians around the world are making these fundamental mistakes, believing because they want to believe, not because it is true.

It is a sure prescription for ignorance, not wisdom.

And it is up to the Christian to be honest with himself as to what this means for his faith.

For me this is the exciting thing about the Falling Higher Power Formula™!!

Let me illustrate this even further in a more advanced way . . .

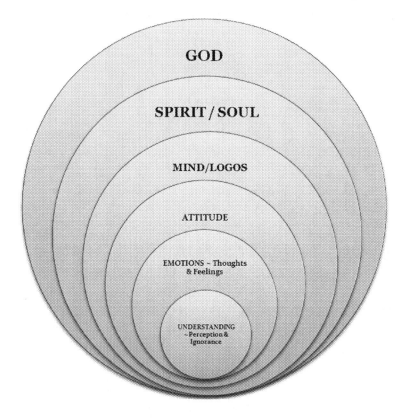

$ = GOD ~ Spirit/Soul

God is the Active and the only Self-Conscious principle, First Cause and the Absolute Essence of all that is!

The Spirit is the vital principle, animating force or energy level back and through all, to reach and understand our ultimate goal—GOD.

The Spirit is the cause of all manifestation on any plane.

The Soul, through which the Spirit operates, are two parts or aspects of the exact same medium, self-existent and co-eternal with one another.

The Soul is the substance of the Spirit and are subjective to it, or it can be considered as the Matter of Spirit.

The Soul simply reflects what the Spirit casts into it.

Although the Spirit is conscious mind and the Soul is subconscious mind and subjective to the Spirit, it is never unconscious, because it has the intelligent ability to consciously work out the commands of the Spirit.

Unlike the Spirit, the Soul cannot analyze, dissect or deny.

The Soul is always impersonal, neutral, passive and receptive.

It neither knows nor care who uses it, but is always creative and ready to work for any or all alike.

It is bound to accept and act as the medium of Thought and Power of the Spirit, always obeying the Law or Will of the Spirit.

Think of the Soul as the soil working on the seed, as the seed is working in the soil.

We may plant carrots and roses with potatoes and weeds, and we shall receive all four plants from the one neutral creative medium which knows neither good nor bad, but is conscious only of its ability to do.

<u>M – Mind</u>

The Mind is the Intelligent Power, the driving force that manifests in the concrete material world all the time in all areas of our lives, positive or negative.

The human mind is a wonderful thing and once a belief is imprinted in our subconscious mind, our conscious mind will find ways to unconsciously attract, delete, generalize and distort information in order to prove that our beliefs is true and will serve us.

The power of the Mind is of the exact same substance as the building blocks of the universe.

The activity in our brains is chemical-magnetic energy and it takes the form of waves.

In fact, as we live through each moment of the day we have brainwaves all the time—sometimes vibrating smaller, sometimes larger—but all the time.

What we send out mentally and spiritually, will return to us.

Be as though you are, and you will be.

That is because creation really is all in the mind.

Where our conscious Mind leads the reality we build will follow.

The outer world is a reflection of our inner world.

What we see outside of us is what has first taken place inside of us.

In our inner world we have infinite potential to enjoy plentiful abundance in all things.

This potential just has to unfold, and that is our decision (choice).

Nothing can happen without it.

If we keep training ourselves to have the mentality that rises above mediocre bigotry, it will release an astonishing power in our lives that can conquer any difficulties.

It will revolutionized our lives if we can learn its secret and how to put it into practice.

At some point spoken words (sound waves) cease to exist because they run into friction and eventually run out of energy.

Mind power never cease to exist because it is not subject to natural laws; it defies time and space.

The human faculty of reason or rationality, associated with thinking, cognition and intellect is the ability of the human mind to form and operate on concepts in abstraction in an ordered and goal-oriented manner.

The mind is the capacity human beings have to make sense of things, to establish and verify facts and to change or justify practices, institutions and beliefs by which rational thinking comes from one idea to a related idea, the understanding about cause and effect, truth and falsehood and good or bad.

It has the ability to self-consciously change beliefs, attitudes, traditions, and institutions and therefore the capacity for freedom, self-determination, thought, opinion, and consideration, due relation, proportion, expectation and analogy.

It is our ability to be able to act as the effective gatekeeper to our own mind which could easily make the difference between succeeding or failing in our endeavours.

We need to strive to keep our mind sets free of negative influences and to focus on creating value in everything we do, should we truly want to become successful in every aspect of our lives.

L – Logos

The original Greek term 'λόγος' logos is the root of the modern English word 'logic'; The logic reasoning of God, or the Word (*) or Will of God.

(*The last four words of John 1:1 (Ͽεὸς ἦν ὁ λόγος, literally 'God was the Logos', or 'God was the Word', have been a particular topic of debate within Christianity. Early New Testament manuscripts did not distinguish upper and lower case, so that pre-existing beliefs about the Trinity have influenced translation. In this construct, the complement (God) and the subject (Logos) both appear in the nominative case, and the complement is therefore usually distinguished by dropping any article and moving it before the verb. Grammatically, the phrase could therefore read either 'the word was god' or 'the word was a god', although many scholars see the movement of 'God' to the front of the clause as indicating an emphasis more consistent with 'God was the Word'.)

Logos is the distinction between Perfect Idea or Intermediary Divine Being active in creation and revelation, necessary to bridge the enormous gap between imperfect matter and material world.

The Logos of God is the bond of everything, holding all things together and binding all the parts and prevents them from being dissolved and separated.

It is an E-mail from God; a text from Heaven.

It's not a checklist or a strategy; It is a state of mind!!

Logos is not *'Chronos'*, like in chronological, sequential or quantitive order; But rather *'Kairos',* like at the right or opportune moment when something special happens.

Paying attention to the Power Within and all around us, rather than sweat or strain and good or bad luck, shapes and molds every moment of our lives and paved the way to change our lives dramatically, make our dreams come true, and create the very kind of life we really want to live.

This means we are getting back on the right path and living our life's purpose.

We are following our heart which means we are finally having the experiences our soul desires.

The Universe is ready to reward us.

God never adds up by human calculation.

But that's not our business anyway, that's God's business.

What do we do when faith seems foolish? What do we do when God doesn't add up?

It's essential to listening to the messages of our Minds.

These messages are our Spirit's desire.

They communicate to us what we are meant to be doing at any given time in our life.

If we don't follow these messages, we will inevitably be straying from our life's path, and it will only get worst.

Our Inner Voice is a gift from a Bigger Power.

When rejecting that kind of gift we are rejecting the Grace that goes with it.

As a result we struggle, we yearn and we starve.

This kind of negativity will constrict the flow of Grace into our life causing pain and emotional starvation.

Oftentimes the situations and people in our life that are causing the most stress and pain are there to remind us that we are not following our hearts.

A – Attitude

'Attitude is everything'

~ Nelson Mandela

Attitude is the window into the mind and the aroma of the heart.

It is the typical behavioral tendency and the root of our emotions and understanding.

Attitude generally constitutes individual degrees of positive or negative views, beliefs or judgments of a person, place, thing or an event.

It is normally a mindset of assumptions, methods or notations which is so established that it creates a powerful incentive to continue to adopt or accept prior behaviors, choices or tools.

Attitude should not be determined by others. That gives them power over us.

We control how we act, our mood, and what we say.

Furthermore comprises attitude of the conscious expression of the will to control the tenor and flow of our chemical-magnetic energy differently.

It constitutes the choice or willingness to take control of our mind and our reality, the only way we can create something out of nothing.

Most people spend more time planning a holiday than they do planning the rest of their lives.

They live by default instead of design; Out of memory instead of imagination.

E – Emotions

Emotions is the gearbox shifting the gears of our minds into action of our reality, positive or negative.

Emotions are highly influenced by our conditioned behavior, perceived experiences, associative learning and belief systems.

It works hand-in-hand with the cognitive process, or the way we think about an issue or situation.

It is the complex psycho-physiological experience of an individual's state of mind as interacting with bio-chemical (internal) and environmental (external) influences.

The term emotion is based on the Latin *'emovere'*, where *e*— (variant of ex-) means 'out' and *'movere'* means 'motion or move'.

Many did not realize until the end that happiness is a choice.

The so-called comfort of familiarity overflowed into our emotions, as well as our physical lives.

We got stayed stuck in old patterns and habits. Fear of change had us pretending to others, and to ourselves, that we are content.

Most people just cannot understand all this.

Because our conditioning tells us that the body is a machine without awareness and that what is in our mind is irrelevant, fanciful, silly, and meaningless and as long as we do not see the connection, we cannot create or attract.

Deep within, we longed to laugh properly and have silliness in our life again.

The only way we can create something out of nothing is by becoming conscious of the power of our emotions, thoughts and feelings.

T – Thoughts

Our thoughts comprises of either positive or negative thinking.

It is the magnifying glass focusing our attitude, emotions and feelings.

Our thoughts constitutes for our mental or intellectual activity involving every individual's Soul, or Subjective consciousness.

To think is to conceive of in the mind or consideration.

It is the intellectual exertion aimed at finding an answer to a question or the solution of a practical problem.

Every thought has its own vibration.

Quantum physics teaches us that we manifest our thoughts as actions.

What we are, depends on what we think, and what we think is what we feel.

What we think habitually will tend to happen.

We become what we are in our thoughts. Positive or negative.

F – Feelings

Positive or negative feelings is the mirror reflecting our thoughts.

It is a state of consciousness; the conscious subjective experience of emotion.

It is clear that our emotions and feelings have physical effects.

We sweat when nervous and we breathe fast when anxious and that proves that our emotions have a direct link with our physical reality.

If the vibration is positive we feel good, happy, strong, and keen to get things done.

If the vibration is negative, we feel low, sad, tired, depressed, stuck and unmotivated.

And yet we still think our bodies and our minds are quite separate.

This could not be further from the truth.

If something is *on our mind*, it is having an effect on our body and our actions, and this means it is influencing our life.

U – Understanding

Understanding is the link between the engine and the wheels.

It is the spiritual human experiences that open a door to knowing, comprehension (wisdom) and knowledge.

Understanding means information gained to deal adequately with a psychological process related to an abstract or physical concept such as a situation, message or person, whereby one is able to think about it and use it, to take in or contain as part of something larger.

It means to grasp the nature, significance or meaning and constantly learning to improve abilities and dispositions with respect to an object of knowledge sufficient to support intelligent behavior.

To me it is GOD's instruction to us to use our potential to the fullest and use it to our great advantage.

Knowledge should be viewed as a branch of Spirituality, concerning an essence of our being and consciousness that transcends physical matter.

Metaphorically this field may be described as an invisible, uniform sea of light and love underlying the Universe.

Thus, it makes perfect sense to learn how to tap into knowledge, to remove resisters and find answers to questions.

P – Perception

Perception is the process of attaining awareness or understanding in the brain's perceptual systems, organizing and interpreting sensory information shaped by learning, memory, illusions, imagined or ambiguous (*) images.

(*Ambiguous ~ more than one possible interpretation; Uncertain nature or significance; No intrinsic or objective meaning; Not organized in conventional patterns; Difficult to understand or classify; Obscure)

Perception is expectations outside conscious awareness.

It underline the mechanisms of the perceiver as sensory maps and demonstrating a stable, active and pre-conscious attempt to make sense of their input even though the sensory information may be incomplete and rapidly varying.

Perspective is a cognitive choice (or the result of this choice) of a context or reference to categorize, codify and cohesively forming a coherent value system.

Perspective is normally associated base values or beliefs regarding situations and/or facts, judging their relative importance and proper ability to see the objectivity or accurate point of view.

We accumulate the learning of a lifetime and stored it inside our subconscious, a mental drawer within our minds.

I believe we can, if we know how, tap into this to get answers to most of our questions.

The energy, positive or negative, associated with every action and every belief and every memory is stored inside right down to cellular level.

It seems that every event in our life leaves its traces in the form of a memory that is stored somewhere inside our subconscious mind.

You see, you are always right no matter what.

You will always find ways to prove that you are right even if it means you must destroy your dreams, your health, your happiness and wealth in the process.

Do you know; More than 95% of our core belief systems were formed before the age of 8 by your parents, peers and authorities.

And they were formed to protect you as a child—but as a grownup most of our childhood beliefs do not serve us anymore.

See how important conditioning and the emotions are?

We can shape our own lives, because on a quantum level there is no time, time does not exist.

We do not need to stick to our conditioned ideas of how long it takes to transform our lives, health, build great wealth, etc.

All that will happen if we are not creating positive energy on the *In-side*, is that we will only put in a lot of exhausting effort and will never get results as good as we could be getting.

I – Ignorance

Ignorance is unawareness or a selective state of being uninformed.

It is the lack of knowledge, education or intelligence; a blank space on a person's mental map.

It is still acceptable if you do not know; but the danger of ignorance lies in the fact that *you do not know that you do not know.*

'Ignorance more frequently begets confidence
than did knowledge'.

Charles Darwin

Imagine this . . . the Mayans had wheeled toys, as well as cattle . . . yet they never hitched the idea to the active principle, harnessing their cattle to wheeled carts.

Imagine . . . we knew how electricity worked, but instead of using the principles that underlie it to put it to our own use, we continued to gaze out of the window passively watching the lightning as it randomly struck the earth.

It is only our ignorance that leads us to consistently ignore the effect of our mind on our life.

Discord, misery and unhappiness are the result of ignorance; the result of the misuse of our true nature.

So if we want to turn our life around or bring in great abundance, health, safety, riches or happiness of any other kind, we have to learn the simple steps of how we manipulating our Mind Power.

We do not have to face up to, or put up, with everything.

We do not have to sweat or strain, believe in good and bad luck or play the lotto.

All we have to learn is to flow our chemical-electromagnetic energy differently, for nothing affects our experience except how we vibrating our energy.

Like attract like ~ it is the universal law.

When something is on our minds, whether we are aware of it or not, has everything to do with the way our life is.

Where our mind leads, our body and the reality we build will follow.

By doing this we will learn how easy it is to be misled by outside influences as a result of ignorance and incorrect mind sets.

9.

A Different Flow Chart

'Every religious book has to be read, not only with the tongue and eyes, but with the truest and purest light which our heart, conscience and intellect can supply us. Though they were true in their original purity, we are not sure of the form which they subsequently took.'

A.Yusaf Ali—The Qur'an

I PERSONALLY THINK THAT ONE does not have to be muscled into what to believe.

We can, and rather should, use our own minds and knowledge.

Again, at this point, I would like to make myself clear that this is *NOT* about blasphemy, ridicule or contempt.

I am not trying to convince anyone that I'm right and they are wrong.

I can only demonstrate to the level of my ability to know.

This is *NOT* about a mysterious religion, heretical cult or accepting any specific religion or their beliefs.

I do not promise something for nothing.

Actually this is not a new thought.

Many of the great thinkers over the centuries had punctuate all of this.

We have the ability to think for ourselves. Our minds matter!

God does not want us to suspend our reasoning powers when clearly confronted with questionable or hopelessly ambiguous information.

Human existence is made up with the capacity for rational thought, a divine attribute of the image of the living God.

Follow me for the just a moment here . . .

Of course, we must reason in all honesty, humility and courageousness and not exalts our human reasoning above clear understanding.

Man does not create; He just uses creation that is already there.

Therefore we can reach the logical conclusion that real faith is free, open and creative.

Christianity should not be a mindless religion.

I challenge my religion because I want to *Reason* out the truth.

In South Africa, *Apartheid* was supposed to be a good idea; but, it did not work.

In Russia, *Communism* was supposed to be a good idea; but, it did not work.

Christianity is a good idea . . . But, so quickly and so tragically we trade in our dirty knees and scraped elbows for combed hair and clean fingernails.

Our tears before God becomes a suit coat and a study guide in the name of spiritual maturity.

The most common and orthodox message from today's emphasis to be Christian is simply to be a *believer* . . .

- Believe in Christ and you have salvation

- Believe in Christ or go to Hell

- Believe literally in the chosen books for the Bible as God's 'Word'

- Obey the rule and creed of the authoritarian Church

Would Jesus recognize his teachings today in the traditional accounts of his ministry?

I think He would however, be heartsick because he stood for something that is mostly missing in these records.

What is missing is fundamentally important to everyone.

Most people preferred the public teachings of today.

But few however accepted the teachings, the theory of nature and the system of logic it justifies.

These accounts have never been fully tested and therefore, unlike anything else, might today be the only way to overcome all of our problems globally.

This give way to a higher civilization based on reasoning lovingly in moderation and sharing.

It is my opinion that we ARE all part of the Divine, God.

I think it is more important constantly seeking God, than sitting on your hands and finding God through certain dogmas or beliefs.

This is not a competition, people!!

I do not claim that I discovered any new truth.

I believe, to suppose that the Creative Intelligence of the universe would create man in bondage and leave him bound, would be to dishonor this Omnipresent Power we call God.

In contrast, it is far more believable for me to seek God through gaining knowledge, rather than just believe.

We can consciously connect to the Divine through creative silence, listening to the vibrating sounds of our inner being.

'We need to find God, who cannot be found in noise and restlessness. God is the friend of silence. See how trees, flowers, grass grows in silence; see how the stars, the moon and the sun moves in silence. We need silence to be able to touch souls.'

Mother Teresa of Calcutta

We all have beliefs.

But I think true believers hear a different message.

We do not *insist,* like the modern school of thought in Christianity, that we have a ring-side seat, or the corner on the final truth interpreting Jesus, the Word of God or for that matter, God.

The message should be more spiritual than religious.

The place to find God is with-In oneself, not in externals like the belief, dogma or dictations of the church.

My interpretation is that we could experience the Power of the Living God, as It is vibrating right through the universe as well as our genes.

Not by a set of correct beliefs or creeds . . .

But by *SEEKING,* and not *FINALIZING* God.

Therefore, it is essential to know ourselves and be touched by what the most of the fundamental scriptures call, the transforming power of love and light.

Seeking God is the true act of faith.

I believe that was the main point of Jesus all along.

One of the dangers in the interactions of the bible is a jading to the raw realities, and our familiarity with who really was involved and the events what happened out there.

These were real people 2000 years ago.

These were not caricatures or symbols or devices manipulated by God to teach future generations, but real, ordinary very-much-like-you-and-me people.

The Bible was written over a 1600 year period.

The difference between the last book in the OT (Micah) and the first book in the NT (Matt) spans 700 years.

All of its writers lived at different times and came from many walks of life.

Kings, judges, prophets, farmers, shepherds and fisherman. The gospel writer Luke was a doctor.

The Bible is a unique book.

At the time when there were wrong ideas about the shape of the earth, the Bible refers to it as a 'circle or sphere' (Isaiah 40:20) and that it 'hangs on nothing' (Job 26:7)

God is a metaphor for life-affirming principles.

Today contemporize physics documents the truth of that principle and the necessity of expanding our present system to include logical reasoning.

Limited to our present system of logic, we will remain predisposed forever to reason judgmentally, when in spirit, we know this is unacceptable.

Much of the evil in the world can be overcome or removed if humanity had embraced our God-given reason from our earliest evolutionary stages.

The laws of nature that we've discovered and learned to use to our advantage that make everything realities have existed eternally, from electricity and computers to cell phones and space travel.

But we have decided we would rather live in superstition and fear instead of learning and gaining knowledge.

It is much more soothing to believe we are not responsible for our own actions than to actually do the hard work required for success.

We can think of this as upgraded intellectual software.

The Power of the Mind expand our consciousness of reality in truly new ways, just as upgraded software expands the potentials of a computer to process data in new ways.

Another way to think of it is like mathematics.

The Mind facilitate a quantum leap into mental space that our present systems cannot access, just like Einstein's mathematics provides the key to entering dimensions of our physical world that traditional laws of mathematics cannot penetrate.

Scientists demonstrate that meditation and prayer can activate areas of the brain in which feelings of bliss, well-being and oneness are processed.

This suggests the brain is capable of processing both analytical and spiritual ideas.

Could it be that nature intends our spiritual thinking to be as clear and concise as our analytical thinking?

Perhaps we have not yet learned how to use these areas of the brain, dedicated spiritual thinking to the fullest potential.

Could this be that Jesus discovered the way to awaken unused portions of our mind?

Jesus was unique among social revolutionaries.

He did not blame existing religious, economic or political institutions.

The revolution he saw was a far deeper one, without which other reforms could only be superficial and transitory.

In simple terms, Jesus revealed a way to elevate our everyday ego to the same level as our spiritual values.

He revealed a fact about the nature of reality that justifies a new method of reasoning which will be in harmony with spiritual principles.

It was in their desperation that people met Jesus.

A lawyer counter his offer of love with riddles, a priest called him a devil and another called him a bastard.

The religious esteemed drag an adulterous girl through the temple with rocks in their hands and murder in their hearts.

A wealthy man walked away.

It is in this instance where the scholar becomes a student, the tough becomes tender, the elegant plead and beg, the sophisticated becomes a fool and the much-too-grown-ups throws all of their polish away for the simple heart of a child.

We are but *one thought* away on this earth from learning a truly new path to the Kingdom of Heaven.

This is the only practical path to a higher civilization, the only way to overcome the prerequisite of evil.

The future will be determined by our choice to act, or not, on this thought.

---◆◇◆---

'Will you be so sure when your day is
near, say you don't believe?
You had the chance but you turned it
down, now you can't retrieve,
Perhaps you'll think before you say that God is dead and gone
Open your eyes, just realize that he's the One'

From the song 'After Forever' by Black Sabbath ~
Ozzy, Geezer, Tony & Bill

---◆◇◆---

10.

What happens to us when we die?

PHI's (pronounced 'Fee') 1.618 to 1 ubiquity in nature clearly exceeds coincidence. Ancient history assumed that the mysterious magic inherent to PHI was written at the beginning of time and must have been proclaimed by the Creator of the Universe as the 'Divine Proportion.'

Dan Brown

DO YOU KNOW; ALMOND nuts were found in the tomb of Tutankhamun, the 11th pharaoh of the 18th dynasty of ancient Egypt?

This suggests that there is a great possibility that almonds were sufficiently valued to be taken on old King Tut's journey to the afterlife.

So why is it still here around on this earth just to be discovered?

The great question *'Why'* has forever been upon man's lips.

Why the sickness, sorrow, suffering and the life-time of trouble only to be met by a grim and sinister tomb?

Few indeed have been able to answer this question.

I believe, however, those few have been passed by unheeded in the struggle for existence in this life.

Mostly all people believe that *something* inside a human being is immortal and survives death.

Death and dying are an inevitable part of human life.

Everyone experiences it, that's the law.

What happens to us when we die?

Do we go to Heaven or do we go to Hell?

People around the world turn to religion to answer questions about death and the afterlife.

Especially when someone is facing with his or her own mortality.

The mystery of death is so profound that, despite the millennia of theories and explanations that exist on the subject in mythology, religious doctrine and scientific research, people today are more confused than ever about it.

Strangely, even a brief glance at many of the world's religions reveals that many theologies glamorize death, promising rewards in the afterlife.

That includes an increased understanding of God and the universe and even, in some cases, supernatural powers that were unavailable during mortal life.

It seems that death is often more attractive than being alive.

All these ideas bring comfort to many people who have lost loved ones or are facing death themselves.

But I, personally, don't believe there is such a *'place'* as Heaven or Hell.

Now, once again I want to make myself perfectly clear.

I do not claim that I have the final say in things, and it is not my intention to try to convince anyone of anything.

But maybe, just maybe, the answer is simpler than anyone think?

> *'I don't know what I may seem to the world, but as to myself, I seem to have been only like a boy playing on the sea shore and diverting myself in now and then finding a smoother pebble or prettier shell than ordinary, whilst the great ocean of truth lay all undiscovered before me'.*

> *Isaac Newton*

In this regard I am too much of a Christian Agnostic.

I regards the question of the existence of life after death as beyond our knowledge.

I do not say there is no afterlife.

I simply state that we do not know.

Alas, we do not know whether the grave is the end of this life; or the door of another; or whether the night here is not somewhere else a dawn.

The brain is the most complex organ in a human being.

The largest part of the brain, the cerebral cortex is estimated to contain 15 to 33 billion neurons, each connected by synapsis to several thousand other neurons.

These neurons communicate with one another by means of signal pulses to distant parts of the brain and/or body, targeting specific recipient cells.

From a philosophical point of view, what makes the brain special in comparison to other organs is that it forms the physical structure associated with the Mind.

> 'Men ought to know that from nothing else but the
> brain come joys, delights, laughter and sports, and
> sorrows, grieves, despondency and lamentations.'

> *Hippocrates*

The mechanisms by which brain activity gives rise to consciousness, thoughts and feelings remain very challenging to understand, despite rapid modern day scientific progress.

Much about how the brain works remains a mystery.

So it is hard to imagine that mankind reached such a high level of consciousness and of our existence, if it were all to end with this life.

There is blindness far worse than not being able to see; a paralysis far worse than legs that are bent and twisted and death far beyond the tomb.

Interestingly enough, scientific research into single-celled organisms at cellular level suggests that the nature of life does not automatically include a self-destruct mechanism.

In other words, it appears that death is an unnatural part of life.

If it so happens that one's existence can end at any time and is not everlasting, it makes one's existence pointless in the first place.

One basic idea in parts of Africa and Asia and throughout the Pacific regions of Polynesia, Melanesia, and Micronesia many believe that the Spirit—not a Soul—is immortal.

In fact, certain languages do not even have the word Soul.

Since each Spirit and Soul is in very aspects part of the Infinite Whole, it leads to the logical conclusion that it is impossible that any Spirit, or Soul for that matter, can be lost.

The laws of God is not of the dead, but of the living . . . !!

Take gravitation for instance. Gravitation is one of God's laws.

Everybody abides to it.

Regardless of who or what we are, rich or poor, powerful or humble, saint or sinner, fat or lean or white or black, the law of gravity works on everybody eternally, inflexibly and infallibly.

Ignorance of these laws excuses no one from its effects.

But by examining and learning to understand ourselves and the Power of the Mind, we can reach escape velocity and enter God's orbit.

The body is a concrete idea, existing in time and space, for the sole purpose of furnishing a vehicle through which Life may express itself.

But the Mind think independently from the body.

It exit our four dimensions of time and space, to God who exists out of it, therefor sealed it forever, even after death.

Study, learn and apply the lessons in the Falling Higher Power Formula™

God/Spirit/Soul = Power of the Mind and Logos ~
Attitude ~
Emotions ~ Thoughts and Feelings
Understanding ~ Perceptions and Ignorance

Many schools of religious thought simply accept the inevitability of death, and offer better alternatives that await the faithful in the afterlife.

It is then a logical conclusion to assume that the Source of all Life, God, would also hold the keys to death.

Without the glue of consciousness the Spiritual dimension essentially reboots.

What have we discovered this far?

- That when man dies, his physical body decays into matter from which it came from

- That the Spirit, or the Soul through which the Spirit proclaims Itself, is the breath, the spark of life, or the heart of the life principle which endows man to be alive

More we could not ask, and more could not be given, than that which has been given from the Infinite God, the Foundation of the Universe.

'Whosoever drink of the water that I shall give him shall never thirst. But the water that I shall give him shall be in him a well of water springing up into everlasting life. The hour come, and now is, when the true worshipers shall worship the God in Spirit and in Truth.'

~ ST. JOHN—Four.

Let us no longer fight the same old fight.

Let us no longer remember that we were once on the outer rim; let us forget the past and live in the Eternal Present.

To-day is good; to-morrow will be even better and that vista of to-morrows that stretches down the bright Eternity of an endless future will all be good.

For the Nature of Reality cannot change.

The Infinity is always at peace because there is nothing to disturb it.

Freedom is just another word for nothing left to lose.

And, Intellectual freedom is only the right to honest truth.

The Mind is conscious union with God.

We cannot escape from the creative Power of our Minds and there is no use in trying to do so.

Therefor there must be a *thinker* that thinks through the brain.

The new birth does not comes by observation nor by loud proclamation, but through an inner Sense of Reality.

We cannot tell where this comes from if we look to outward things, as it proceeds from the innermost parts of our own being.

This is in line with the idea on quantum level, the Truth knows neither yesterday, to-day nor to-morrow.

Heaven is not a *place*, but a state of mind.

We must be lifted up, that is, we must realize our divine nature and relationship to the Omnipotent God.

This relationship is one of complete Unity.

For the average person immortality means to that man shall persist after the experience of physical death, retaining a full recollection of himself and the ability to continue as a self-conscious personality.

This means he must carry with him a complete remembrance.

Man, then, if he is to have an immortality worthy of the name, must continue, as he now is, beyond the grave.

Eternal Life can know no death, so it follows that death is no part of God, Who knows nothing about death.

Thus the law of the Spirit makes us free from death: the law of the Spirit is freedom and knows no bondage.

Perhaps that means we can only die from one dimension or plane to another.

Our Spirit can be compared to an individual drop of water and when we die, our Spirit maintains the identity of God, flowing forever in the river of the Omnipresent Spirit, continuously and eternally part of the One.

The facts are conclusive that we have a Spiritual body now, and do not have to die to receive one.

The Life Principle viewed matter only as death, but viewed as life and Unity it becomes life everlasting.

We come into everlasting life as we elevate this Inner Principle to a sense of the Unity of man with God.

> *'Niagara fills the heavens with its song. Man will arrest the falling flood. He will change its force to electricity, that is to say, to light.'*

> *Robert Green Ingersoll*

This means that with-In our present bodies, at the center of the earth and throughout all space, there is a Substance more than the bodies which we see.

This idea is very far-reaching; it shows that we might have a *body* right within the physical one, which could be as real as the one of which we are accustomed to.

If the Infinitive has molded the outer body in form, why should It not also mold the inner one in a continuous state of flow?

Strange as it may seem, we do not have the same physical bodies that we had a few months ago.

New particles have taken the place of the old; our bodies have completely changed into a new one.

The only reason why they have taken the same form is that the Infinite has provided the same mold.

We now can see ourselves as we really are.

The resurrection *body*, then, will not have to be snatched from some cosmic shelf as the soul soars aloft, but is found to exist already with-In us.

The birth of the Spirit into the light is an awakening to the realization that God has been with-In us all the time, forever held in the bosom of the Universe, Sons of God, Sons of freedom and not of bondage.

Today is the day of complete salvation.

Not tomorrow or the day after, or in the hereafter, but in the NOW.

It is that Creation which, while it may have beginnings and ends, of It-self neither begins nor ends.

God's love is complete in us, we are just what we are, and what we must be, because of True Nature.

In the new schools of thought there are those who claim to demonstrate only by the Spirit; and those who claim to demonstrate only by the Mind.

This is a distinction which is suppositional rather than real and is impossible, because, if there were two powers, we would at once have duality and our philosophy of Unity would be contradicted.

At death consciousness is gone, and so too the continuity in the connection of times and places.

Without consciousness, space and time are nothing; in reality we can take any time—whether past or future—as your new frame of reference.

Death is just a reboot that leads to all potentialities.

The belief in duality has given rise in theology to the idea of a God and a Devil, each with powers to impose upon man a blessing or a curse.

This monstrous thought is robbing men of their birthright to happiness and a sense of security.

Even today men still openly teach that there is an evil power in the universe, that there is damnation to the souls of those who do not fall down and worship; what, they do not know.

But the time is rapidly coming when such teachings will be thrown on the scrap heap and numbered among the delusions of a frantic mentality.

It has been the habit of many religious teachers of all times to hold the crowd in awe before a mighty throne of condemnation and utter destruction till the poor, ignorant population have rent the air with their lamentations of complete despair.

This, indeed, is a good method to compel the attention with the hope of salvation through some sacred rites to be performed by those whom 'God' had appointed.

In justice to such an awful performance, we would better give to these religious teachers the benefit of the doubt and say that they themselves have believed in the atrocious teachings which they have so unhesitatingly given out.

Be this as it may, the time has now come for a clearer understanding of the true nature of the true One, in which I believe and seek to reason and understand.

That there could be a God of vengeance and hate, having all the characteristics and personal traits of a huge man in a terrible rage, no person can well believe in and keep his sanity.

I will say, then, and without mincing matters in the least, that the most I had better believe about such a God, is that there is no such being.

As the belief in the duality of God and Devil, has robbed theology of its greater message, so it has robbed much of the philosophy of the ages of a greater truth.

For the belief in duality has created a confusion that is almost as great as that in theology.

It has made a philosophy of good and evil in which men have come to believe.

True philosophy in every age, however, has perceived that the Power back of all things must be One Power.

The clear thought of Unity shone forth as a beacon light toward which weary souls have traveled hoping to find reality.

We owe the great philosophers of all times the advancement of the world; For they have been the great way-showers of mankind.

The Ultimate Cause back of all things must be One, since Life cannot be divided against Itself; the Infinite must be One, for there could not be two infinites.

Everything is in a constant state of flow; it all comes from One source, and will eventually return to that source.

Whatever change takes place must take place within the One that is Changeless; for, being One and Only, It cannot change into anything but Itself.

All seeming change, then, is really only the play of Life upon Itself; and all that happens must happen by and through it.

The Spirit must go forth into creation through law and action.

Life must enter living, and God must flow through man if there is to be a real representation of the Divine through the human.

Each live his own life, within the One Life; it is the Universal Principle.

We are in the Truth when we live in harmony with It; there is no mystery about this, it is common sense.

When we are on our deathbed, what others think of us will be a long way from our mind.

How wonderful, though, to be able to let go and smile long before we are dying.

The key is to understand the nature of evil.

Evil is the main risk factor for happiness.

It is not sufficient to deny, avoid, or ignore evil; it must be understood.

It is not enough to ask God to remove the evil, we must find out why it is there, and what lesson it has for us.

So instead of complaining about these things that trap us, learn about the trap we are in, why we are in it and how it keeps us stuck.

Evil is not an abstract *something* outside one-self.

It is an experience in our own mind.

And by patiently examining and rectifying our minds, we will be gradually led into the discovery of the origin and nature of evil, which will necessarily be followed by its complete eradication.

All evil is corrective and remedial, and is therefore not permanent.

It is rooted in perceptions and ignorance.

Ignorance of the true nature and relation of things, and so long as we remain in that state of ignorance, we remain subject to evil.

There is no evil in the universe which is not the result of ignorance, and which would not, if we were ready and willing to learn its lesson, lead us to higher wisdom.

But men remain in evil, and it does not vanish because men are not willing or prepared to learn the lesson which it came to teach them.

Evil is the absence of the Eternal Good, the absence of the Omnipotent Light.

Evil is really just the extent to which we shut ourselves out from the light of God's presence and love.

Just as light always floods the universe, and darkness is only a mere speck or shadow cast by a small body intercepting a few rays of the illimitable light.

So the Light of the Supreme Good is the positive and life-giving power which floods the universe, and evil the insignificant shadow cast by the self that intercepts and shuts off the illuminating rays which strive for entrance.

Know, then, when the dark night of sorrow, pain, or misfortune settles down upon our souls, and we stumble along with weary and uncertain steps, that we are merely intercepting our own personal desires between ourselves and the boundless light of joy and bliss, and the dark shadow that covers us is cast by none and nothing but ourselves.

And just as the darkness without is but a negative shadow, an unreality which comes from nowhere, goes to nowhere, and has no abiding dwelling-place, so the darkness within is equally a negative shadow passing over the evolving and Light-born soul.

Evil is a lesson to help us grow, and when its lessons are learned, it passes.

But it is possible to refuse to grow and stay in darkness.

Rather learn and take responsibility in a pro-active way.

But I can be sure that where ignorance remains, and I am not aware of it, a lesson may be in order.

A person may shut themselves up in a dark room, and deny that the light exists, but it is everywhere without, and darkness exists only in their own little room.

So we may shut out the Light of Truth, or we may begin to pull down the walls of prejudice, self-seeking and error which we have built around ourselves and so let in the glorious and Omnipresent Light.

By earnest self-examination strive to realize, and not merely hold as a theory, that evil is a passing phase, a self-created shadow.

That all our pains, sorrows and misfortunes have come to us by a process of undeviating and absolutely perfect law.

Have come to us because we deserve and require them, and that by first enduring, and then understanding them, we may be made stronger, wiser and nobler.

When we have fully entered into this realization, we will be in a position to mold our own circumstances, to transmute all evil into good, and to weave, with a master hand, the fabric of our destiny.

'Sometimes when I'm alone, I wonder aloud
If you're watching over me, Some place far abound
I must reverse my life, I can't live in the past
Then set my soul free, Belong to me at last'

From the song 'Cemetery Gates' by Pantera ~
Phillip; Diamond; Rex; Vinnie

Conclusion

'It is not in the stars to hold our destiny, but in ourselves.'

William Shakespeare

OUR LIVES ARE HEAVILY influenced by the way we think and how our subconscious mind has been conditioned through life's experiences.

If there is a Divine Creator, GOD, way up there in *Heaven* at some couple o' trillion x 9,460,800,000,000 kilometer, it seems, ***to me at least***, like shooting arrows at random in the dark in the hope to hit the target.

But, GOD is also with-In us.

It is really possible for God to be both in *Heaven* as well as *In-Side* us; AND *In Between.*

We have been conditioned to allow all sorts of mental programming to affect our lives without even being aware of the damage which this does to our mental state.

But to Think, to Reason, to Grasp and Understand with our *MINDS* great design and purpose in the natural and spiritual world around us, is the key to the answer.

Once we realize the significance of the Falling Higher Formula™ as a launch-pad for a meaningful and rewarding life, it will change our lives.

This is what Life is all about!!

The Falling Higher Formula ™

$$\$ = M \left(\sqrt[4]{E^{t_f} U^{p_i}} \right) L$$

GOD [Spirit/Soul] = Mind & Logos
(Attitude, Emotions—Thoughts & Feelings,
Understanding—Perceptions and Ignorance)

These principles are built into every human being.

In my opinion, these unseen Power of the Mind that comes through alignment with the Powerful Forces created in the universe is by far our most important tool.

All people are fortunate to have this most powerful tool already honed and operating.

It is rather an objective body of knowledge to sustain a personal faith that can deepen, transform and affirm the way many of us are today.

We need to elevate our reasoning *Mind* to the same level as our spiritual thoughts and thus harmonizes our reasoning with our *Spirit*.

This means we can learn to choose the role our Spiritual Nature manifested in the concrete, material world all the time and what reality is by understanding and willingly taking responsibility for our own minds.

We ARE all part of the Divine, God.

Our future will be determined by our choice to act, or not, on this thought.

We will be *FALLING HIGHER!!*

AND I believe this from the bottom of my Heart, Soul and *Mind*.

'Say right or say wrong, outcast yet I belong
I'm high or I'm dry, say I am weak yet I am strong
I am my alter ego, I am subconsciously
In depth but also shallow, Or somewhere in between'

From the song 'In Between' by Judas Priest ~
Tipton; Downing; Hill; Owens; Travis

Author Biography

Andre J. Nel was born February 1958 in the Republic of South Africa.

After graduation from High School, he specialized for several years in Law-Enforcement as Community Re-Integration Officer and Supervisor Religious Care.

He acquired a Bachelor of Art Degree in Criminology and Penology, and several acknowledgements towards his Bachelor in Theology Degree, as well as a FIS accredited Bachelor Degree in Operations Management in the USA.

He currently reside in Jamestown, North Dakota, USA.